Fokker Dr. I in action

By Heinz J. Nowarra

Color by Don Greer
Illustrated by Perry Manley

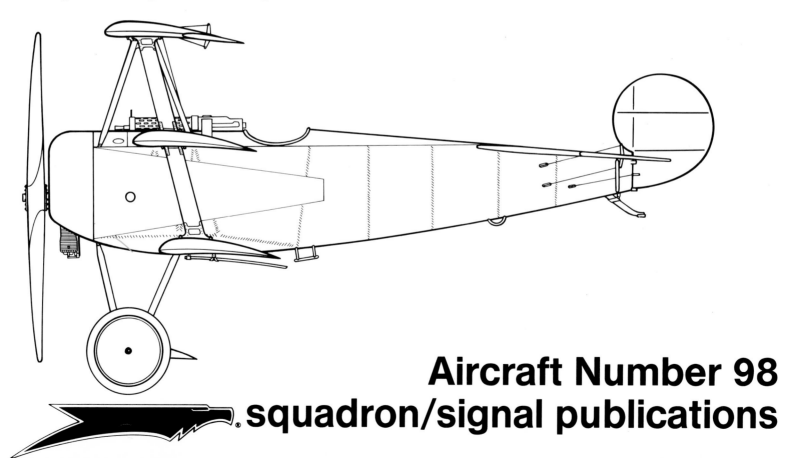

Aircraft Number 98
squadron/signal publications

This Fokker Dr. I (404/17) was flown by Adolf Ritter von Tutschek, an ace with twenty-seven victories, while assigned to *Jasta* 12. He was killed in action on 15 March 1918 during an engagement with SE-5s of No 24 Squadron, RFC.

ISBN 0-89747-229-2

If you have any photographs of the aircraft, armor, soldiers or ships of any nation, particularly wartime snapshots, why not share them with us and help make Squadron/Signal's books all the more interesting and complete in the future. Any photograph sent to us will be copied and the original returned. The donor will be fully credited for any photos used. Please send them to:

Squadron/Signal Publications, Inc.
1115 Crowley Drive.
Carrollton, TX 75011-5010.

Acknowledgements

A special thank you to Mr. Randy Wilson for providing information on his Fokker Dr. I replica.

Photo Credits

Unless otherwise indicated, all photos come from the author's collection.

This Fokker Dr. I (152/17) was the aircraft Manfred von Richthofen used to score his sixty-sixth victory. The combat report says that this aircraft had a Red top wing, Red engine cowling, Red wheels and a Red tail. The fuselage was Green with Red sides beginning just behind the cockpit and running to the tail.

INTRODUCTION

On 15 July 1917 Manfred von Richthofen, commander of *Jagdgeschwader*, recovering sufficiently from his head injury received in an early combat, left the hospital, together with LT Kurt Wolff, and returned to his unit. During his talks with the pilots of *Jastas* 4, 6, 10 and 11 he said, "You will soon be receiving new Fokker triplanes. They climb like monkeys and maneuver like devils." This was the first time many of the pilots had heard of the radical new fighter that they would soon be flying — the Fokker Dr. I.

Prior to this time the German Army Air Service was flying aircraft built primarily by Albatros. Albatros, which had its great success with the Albatros D. I and D. II during 1916, had experienced trouble in producing a new development of these single seat fighters. Thelen and Schubert, who were responsible for design and construction of Albatros fighters, had created the D. III as the German answer to the French Nieuport 11 and 17. The aircraft, however, suffered from structural weakness which caused a number of fatal accidents in front line service.

One cause was the weight of the Mercedes in-line engine. This weight gave the D. III a high diving speed which over stressed the upper wing, causing it to fail in flight. Since its foundation, Albatros, the largest German aircraft manufacture, had a priority on engines produced by the Daimler Engine Works in Stuttgart-Untertuerkheim. This, plus the fact that the Oberusel Factory, which produced copied French rotary engines, was under the control of Anthony Fokker, their greatest competitor, left the designers little choice than to stay with the in-line engines.

Albatros engineers tried to strengthen the wing construction of the D. III, (and its successor the D.V) by the addition of extra bracing struts and wires; however, these modifications did not prove successful. Every German fighter pilot knew that diving and steep turns with an Albatros fighter could be very dangerous and lead to structural failure. When the announcement came that Fokker was working on a triplane fighter, German pilots greeted the news enthusiastically.

Anthony Fokker, a Dutch national, had become one of the primary designers of fighter aircraft for the German Army Air Service. He had begun development of the triplane after the British introduced the Sopwith Triplane into service over the front. In April of 1917, the British No 1 (Naval) Squadron had re-equipped with the Sopwith Triplane, a fighter which quickly proved that it outclassed the Albatros D. III completely. Richthofen reported that, "the Sopwith Triplane is the best aircraft that the enemy possesses. It climbs better, is more maneuverable, and does not lose altitude in a bank. It is faster and can be dived straight down."

Soon after the Sopwith Triplane began combat operations over the front, one example fell into German hands and was immediately transported to the *Inspection der Fliegertruppe (IdFlieg)* in Adlershof near Berlin. It was tested in mock dogfights with an Albatros D.V. MAJ Siegert, Chief of *IdFlieg*, was shocked at its performance and maneuverability and urgently requested that a triplane fighter be designed for the German Army Air Service to counter the Sopwith.

Fokker immediately began designing his answer to the *IdFlieg* request. Fokker's original V.3 triplane prototype emerged as a cantilever triplane powered by a 100 hp, 9 cylinder air cooled Oberursel rotary engine. It was a small aircraft with a wing span of 22 feet, a length of 17 ¾ feet, a height of 10 ½ feet and a top speed of 114 mph. The cantilever design of the uneven wings cut down on drag by eliminating the traditional bracing struts and wires between the wings. The wing design, however, proved prone to vibration and after initial testing, Fokker decided not to offer it to the *IdFlieg* for evaluation.

The Fokker V.3 was the initial triplane fighter prototype built by Fokker. The aircraft had cantilever wings which featured no interplane struts or bracing wires between the wings. The V.3 was a Silver-Gray color and carried no armament.

Tests with the V.3 proved that the wings were strong enough to delete the usual interplane struts; however, service pilots were unhappy with the amount of wing flex and vibration of the unbraced wings.

Fokker's next experimental triplane was given the Fokker designation V.4 and had a longer span wing with interplane struts between the wings to eliminate vibration. The V.4 had a wing span of 23 ¼ feet, a length of 18 ½ feet, and a height of 8 ¾ feet. Empty weight was 855 pounds and loaded weight was 1,287 pounds. The V.4 also had a modification to the horizontal stabilizers. The rounded leading edge used on the V.3 was changed to a straight edge with rounded tips. Tests conducted during early July of 1917 at Adlershof revealed the prototype had a top speed of 111.84 mph. The flight testing at Adlershof ran smoothly and on 14 July 1917 the aircraft was ordered into production as the Fokker F.I (102/17) and a contract for twenty fighters was issued. This small initial production run was in normal *IdFlieg* policy, which delayed mass production of new designs until they had completed service trials under combat conditions.

After three production F.Is were completed (serial numbers F.I 101/17, 102/17 and 103/17) the *IdFlieg* changed the aircraft's designation to Dr. I in keeping with the class designation it had established for triplane, single seat fighters.

(Right) The second triplane fighter prototype, the Fokker V.4, was fitted with interplane struts between the wings. Ailerons were installed on the top wing only. The span of all three wings was unequal, with the top wing having the longest span.

The V.4 prototype was armed with two 7.92MM LMG 08/15 air cooled machine guns and was tested intensively at the *IdFlieg* in Adlershof. The rate of climb and maneuverability of the triplane impressed the pilots who flew the prototype.

Wing And Tail Plane Evolution

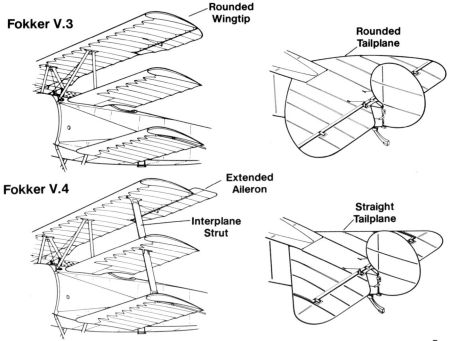

Fokker V.3

Rounded Wingtip

Rounded Tailplane

Fokker V.4

Extended Aileron

Interplane Strut

Straight Tailplane

Development

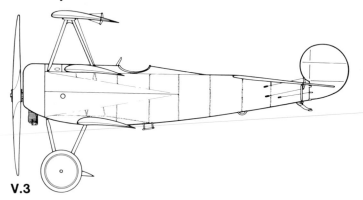

V.3

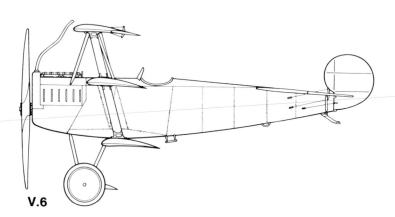

V.6

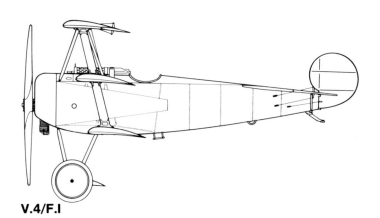

V.4/F.I

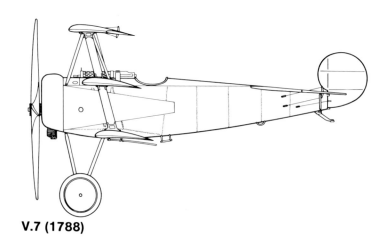

V.7 (1788)

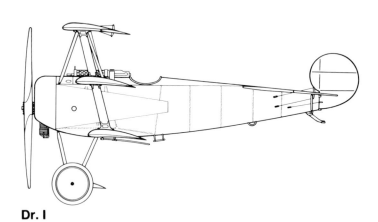

Dr. I

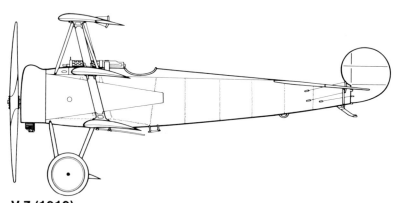

V.7 (1919)

Fokker Dr. I

One of the three F.Is, F.I 101/17, remained at the Fokker factory at Schwerin-Goerries, while the other two, 102/17 and 103/17, were delivered to *Jagdgeschwader 1* at Marckebeeke in Flanders on 19 August 1917, where General Ludendorf inspected both triplanes. Both aircraft were quickly claimed by two of the *Jagdgeschwader* commanders, von Richthofen and Voss. Experience with the first two Fokker F.Is revealed that the aircraft had a tendency to dip a wing during taxing and landings. To protect the wingtip from damage, production Dr. Is had a wooden skid attached to the underside of each wingtip. This was the only external difference between the Fokker F.I and the Dr. I.

Production of the Dr. I was slow to begin and by the time the first batch of six aircraft arrived at the front during mid-October of 1917 both of the original F.Is had been lost in combat. A second batch of eleven arrived a few days after the first group and by the end of October, seventeen aircraft were on strength.

The production Fokker Dr. I was of mixed wood and metal construction. The wings had wooden box spars and compressed plywood ribs which were internally braced with wire. The wing leading edge was covered with plywood, with the remainder of the wing being fabric covered with a wire feathered trailing edge. The wings had no external bracing wires, except for two cross-wires between the steel tube inverted V cabane struts. The top wing was fitted with balanced ailerons which extended past the wing tips. The ailerons were made of steel tubing and covered with doped fabric. Over the course of Dr. I production, the shape of the aileron's inboard edge varied considerably; some being rounded, while others were angular.

The middle wing had two cut outs on both sides of the fuselage to improve the pilot's downward view. The interplane struts were of wooden construction with metal attachment points. The rudder and tail plane were of steel tube construction, with the rudder hinged from the extreme rear of the fuselage. The tailplane was fixed to the fuselage top frame and the elevators were internally balanced.

The fuselage was of welded steel tube construction, braced internally by diagonal bracing wires. It was fabric covered except for two triangular plywood fillets that ran from the engine cowling to a point just behind the cockpit. The fillet was installed to blend the round cowling into the box constructed fuselage and improve the aircraft streamlining. The engine cowling fully enclosed the engine to a point just below the propeller hub and had two circular ventilation holes above and on either side of the propeller hub.

The normal power plant for the Dr. I was the 110 hp Oberursel rotary engine; however, service pilots often replaced the engine with captured French 110 hp Le Rhone engines. One such pilot, LT Werner Voss (who was killed flying F.I 103/17) had a a 110 HP Le Rhone engine installed in the aircraft which had been taken from a British Nieuport fighter! German pilots preferred the French rotary engines because they were more reliable than the Oberursel-built copies.

The triplane's armament consisted of two 7.92MM LMG 08/15 machine guns mounted on the fuselage just in front of the cockpit and synchronized to fire through the propeller arc (LMG means *Luftgekühltes Maschinen-Gewehr* — air cooled machine gun). The guns were fed from two ammunition boxes on either side of the fuselage, each holding 500 rounds of ammunition.

The undercarriage was of welded steel tube construction with the wheels attached to a single elastic cord sprung axle. The axle was encased in an airfoil shaped fairing that ran between the main wheel struts.

Production Dr. Is had a wing span of 23 feet 7 inches, a length of 18 feet 11 inches and a height of 9 feet 8 inches. Empty weight was 894 pounds and full loaded weight was 1,291 pounds. The Dr. I was not a fast fighter, with a top speed of 105 mph; however, it excelled in rate of climb. Time to climb to 13,000 feet was ten minutes, for an initial rate of climb of some 1,300 feet per minute. Service ceiling was approximately 23,000 feet, while the range was 185 miles.

Contemporary Allied fighters were all faster than the Dr. I. The Sopwith Camel had a top speed of 112 mph, the Nieuport 27 had a speed of 106.8 mph and the SPAD VII was far faster, with a top speed of 131 mph. But, as Fokker himself said, "The Fokker Triplane climbed so well and was so maneuverable, that nobody remarked on how slow it was."

Fokker in the cockpit of one of the three F.Is built. Fokker personally tested the F.I intensively. Standing beside him is Reinhold Platz, who was responsible for turning Fokker's designs into final construction drawings.

The F.I (103/17) flown by LT Voss had a face painted on the engine cowling. It has been reported that the aircraft assigned to *Jasta* 10 had Yellow noses; however, if this is correct, the color must have a very dark Reddish Yellow. In all likelihood, the cowling is in Olive Green, the same color used to paint the aircraft's uppersurfaces.

During August of 1917, the Commanding General of the 4th Army visited *Jagdeschwader* and LT Kurt Wolff demonstrated the F.I to the General. Wolff is in the cockpit of F.I 102/17 while Richthofen listens to him briefing the general on the performance of the new triplane.

Wingtip Skid

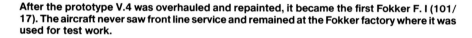

After the prototype V.4 was overhauled and repainted, it became the first Fokker F. I (101/17). The aircraft never saw front line service and remained at the Fokker factory where it was used for test work.

Fokker F. I

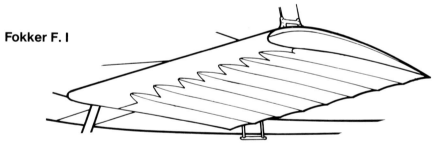

Fokker Dr. I

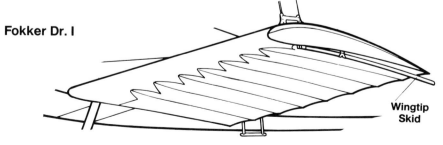

Wingtip Skid

8

This Fokker Dr. I (157/17) was assigned to *Jagdgeschwader* 1, the first German unit to receive the Dr. I. *Jagdeschwader* had a priority on deliveries of the new Fokker triplane fighter.

Since this triplane is painted in 1915 style insignia, it is believed to be part of the initial production batch of sixteen triplanes delivered to the German Army Air Service during early 1917.

The Dr. I differed from the F.I in having wingtip skids under each wingtip. These skids prevented damage to the wingtip during landings and taxiing caused by the Dr. I's tendency to dip a wing. (IdFlieg)

Although this Fokker Dr. I (154/17) was built during 1917, it has been painted with the earlier style *Patee* cross (also know as the Iron Cross) national insignia which had been changed during 1915 to the straight *Balkankreuz*.

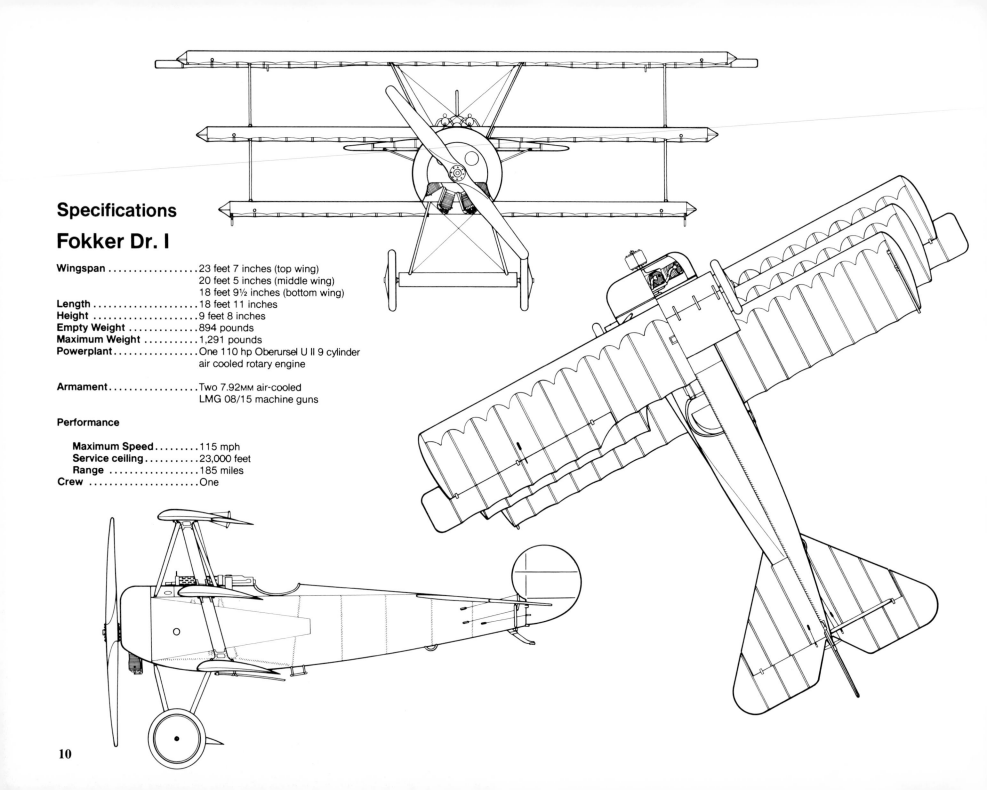

Specifications

Fokker Dr. I

Wingspan . . . . 23 feet 7 inches (top wing)
20 feet 5 inches (middle wing)
18 feet 9½ inches (bottom wing)
Length . . . . 18 feet 11 inches
Height . . . . 9 feet 8 inches
Empty Weight . . . . 894 pounds
Maximum Weight . . . . 1,291 pounds
Powerplant . . . . One 110 hp Oberursel U II 9 cylinder
air cooled rotary engine

Armament . . . . Two 7.92мм air-cooled
LMG 08/15 machine guns

Performance

Maximum Speed . . . . 115 mph
Service ceiling . . . . 23,000 feet
Range . . . . 185 miles
Crew . . . . One

Into Combat

On 7 September 1917 Manfred von Richthofen commander of *Jagdgeschwader 1.*, flying Fokker F.I (102/17), scored the first recorded victory for the Fokker triplane when he shot down a British RE-8 reconnaissance aircraft. Shortly after scoring this victory, von Richthofen departed on an extended leave. While he was gone, LT Kurt Wolff flew the F.I. While at home on 15 September, von Richthofen received a message that LT Wolff had been killed in action in a dogfight with British Sopwith Camels over Wervicq. The triplane was totally destroyed.

The second F.I (F.I 103/17) was flown by LT Werner Voss, commander of *Jasta 10.* While Richthofen was on leave, the Austrian Crown Prince visited *Jagdgeschwader 1* and *Jasta 10.* Voss proudly presented his Fokker to the Crown Prince and the accompanying Chief of *IdFlieg*, MAJ Siegert.

The units comprising *Jagdgeschwader 1* were responsible for testing the early Fokker triplanes in combat and LT Voss lost no time in getting the triplane into action. On 28 August he made his first operational flight with F.I 103/17 and scored a kill over a British aircraft. Although there are no official records of exactly how many victories Voss scored while flying the F.I triplane, according to the war diaries of JG 1, Voss scored seven kills with the F.I between 3 and 23 September 1917.

The combat career of LT Voss was cut short on 23 September 1917 when he became engaged in a running fight with six British SE-5 fighters flown by some of the Royal Flying Corps top aces including CAPT James McCudden. After a long fight, during which he hit every one of the opposing British fighters, Voss was shot down by CAPT Rhys-Davids. The triplane fell near St. Julien, within the British lines, and was captured. Upon inspection of the wreckage, it was discovered that Voss had a French engine, captured from the British, installed in his triplane.

During mid-October of 1917, the first production six Fokker Dr. Is arrived to be followed a few days later by another batch of eleven aircraft. This gave the *Jagdgeschwader* a strength of seventeen Fokker Dr. Is; however, these aircraft would have a short initial combat career.

On 30 October 1917 the Fokker Dr. I suffered a severe setback to its operational career. LT Gontermann, commander of *Jasta 15*, had received one of the first production Dr. Is (115/17). Gontermann, who was a winner of the "Blue Max," wrote in his diary: " I hope that we may have more success than the Richthofen squadron, where Wolff and Voss have been killed on it." His premonition proved correct and on 30 October 1917 he was performing aerobatics at 1,500 feet over his airfield when the Dr. I went out of control and crashed. LT Gontermann was severely injured and died of his injuries the next day.

Observers who had witnessed the crash reported that they had seen the fabric break loose from upper wing and the aircraft begin to break up in the air. The same day Manfred von Richthofen, flying with his brother Lothar, crashed in Fokker Dr. I 114/17. On the following day LT Pastor of *Jasta 11*, who just had joined the unit, crashed to death in Fokker Dr. I. 121/17. All of these crashes were found to be caused by structural failure of the upper wing aileron which led to a total failure of the upper wing.

The rash of crashes cast doubt on the triplane's construction and the aircraft was grounded while *IdFlieg* experts conducted a thorough investigation. The cause of the crashes was found to be aileron failure, followed by disintegration of the upper wing. The underlying cause of the aileron failure was found to be excessive moisture in the wing interior which loosened the glued joints. In one official report the crash commission stated that on inspection of three operational Fokker Dr. Is, the glued joints showed such deterioration that "...the whole wing has lost its structure."

While the triplanes were grounded, the *Jadgeschwader* reverted to Albatros D.Va fighters, although the pilots all hoped that the fix for the wing problem would be found quickly and the triplanes returned to them.

To solve the problem, twelve modifications to the upper wing were ordered including a new aileron attachment and the requirement that all interior wooden wing components were to have a coating of Marine grade varnish to protect them from the weather. The grounding was a serious setback for Fokker, and in all probability cost the designer further orders for the Dr. I. Instead of receiving additional orders for the triplane, Fokker now had to use up his profits to have the wings modified. Additionally, while the modified wing was externally identical to the earlier wing, it was some seven and three quarter pounds heavier that the original wing.

The grounding order was finally rescinded on 28 November 1917 and the Dr. I was again cleared for combat. Deliveries of the Dr. I with the modified wing began in December; however, by that time the tactical surprise offered by the triplane's spectacular performance had been lost.

Approximately 320 Fokker Dr. Is were built and these aircraft were used in action between September of 1917 and June of 1918. After June of 1918, most triplanes left on strength with the German Army Air Service were being used as trainers for the Fokker D. VIII.

German mechanics prepare to pull the propeller of F.I 103.17 through to start the engine. LT Werner Voss is sitting in the cockpit ready for another mission. The F.I lacked the wing tip skids that were added to the production Dr. I.

11

In combat, German pilots viewed the triplane as the best dog-fighter of the war, superior to the Spad VII and Sopwith Camel in close combat. The main combat weakness of the Dr. I was the low power and low compression of its engine. While a program was started to find a superior engine for the Dr. I, none of the re-engined Dr. Is were ever put into production.

The following units were fully or partly equipped with Dr. Is: In the area of operations under the 4th German Army; *Jastas* 7, 28, 29, 30, 47, 51, 52 and 57. In the 17th Army operational area; *Jagdgeschwader 3* with *Jastas* 2, 26, 27 and 36. Also *Jastas* 35, 58, 59 and *Jagdgeschwader 1 (Jastas* 4, 65, 10 and 11). Along the 2nd Army front; *Jastas* 5, 16, 37, 46, 54, and 56. Under the 18th Army were, *Jagdgeschwader 2* with *Jasta* 12, 13, 19, and *Jastas* 8, 15, 22, 24, 44, 48, 53, 69 and 79.

The desperate fighting following the German offensive of 1918 saw the loss of a number of well known German triplane pilots. LT Josehim Wolf (33 victories) of *Jasta 11*, crashed with a broken wing in Dr. I 155/17. LT Mohnicke (9 victories) and LT Just (6 victories) were lost flying Dr. Is. In March of 1918, the commander of *Jagdgeschwader 2* CAPT Ritter von Tutschek (27 victories) fell in action flying Dr. I 404/17. He went down over Braucourt, south of Laon, on 18 March. Lothar von Richthofen crashed with another triplane after a hard fight near Awoingt.

Manfred von Richthofen scored his sixty-sixth victory on 18 March flying Dr. I 152/17. A little more than a month later, he made his last flight, being shot down on 20 April 1918 flying Dr. I 425/17. Although it is widely believed that Dr. I 425/17 was painted overall bright Red, there are claims that the aircraft was actually painted Red on the fuselage and wing uppersurfaces, with pale Blue wing and tailplane undersurfaces.

Jagdgeschwader 1 flew the triplane into the early Summer of 1918 although by this time the triplane was rapidly being replaced by the far superior Fokker D. VII. Some German aces, however, still preferred the triplane to the faster but less maneuverable D. VII. Josef Jacobs kept two Black triplanes as his personal aircraft until September of 1918, even though the rest of his unit was equipped with Fokker D. VIIIs.

As more powerful and faster Allied fighters began appearing over the front, the triplane's slow speed and overall poor performance at higher altitudes quickly brought the front line career of the Dr. I to a close. Problems with those that remained led a great many pilots to state that flying the Fokker was "...hardly worthwhile." The problems were not with the aircraft; they stemmed from the poor quality of the *ersatz* (synthetic) castor oil used to lubricate the engines. During the warmer months, engine overheating and failures became common.

After June of 1918, the remaining Fokker Dr. Is were used primarily as trainers to help transition pilots from in-line engined fighters into the rotary engined Fokker D. VIII.

LT Werner Voss inspects a 110 hp Le Rhone rotary engine (Serial No. 6247) which had been taken from a British Nieuport fighter. This engine was later repaired and installed on his triplane (F.I 103/17).

This F.I (103/17) was flown by LT Werner Voss, commander of *Jasta 10*. Voss was killed flying this triplane when he single handedly engaged a flight of six Royal Flying Corps SE-5s on 23 September 1917.

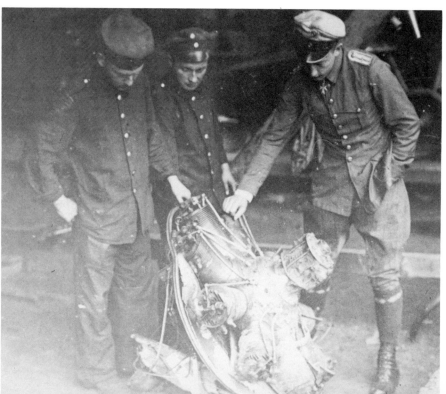

(Above) The Fokker F.I 102/17 on its first test flight from Schwerin-Görries. It is believed that Anthony Fokker conducted this flight personally. Fokker was a gifted pilot who had the respect of many of Germany's best fighter pilots.

Squadron personnel gather around the Fokker F.I flown by Voss. The aircraft had a Silver Gray fuselage and was nicknamed "The Silver Triplane." (From right) Bodenschatz; von Döhring; CAPT Wilberg, Commander of the flying units attached to the 4th Army; Crown Prince Karl; and MAJ Siegert of *IdFlieg*.

(Below) During early August of 1917, the Austrian Crown Prince Karl visited *Jagdgeschwader* 1 and *Jasta* 10. (from left) *Oblt.* von Döhring, representing Richthofen; Bodenschatz, Richthofen's adjudant, LT Krefft, unit technical officer; LT Voss, commander of *Jasta* 10; and Crown Prince Karl. The triplane in the background is F.I 103/17 assigned to LT Voss.

13

Manfred von Richthofen discusses the merits of the triplane with a fellow pilot of *Jasta* 11. He flew Fokker F.I 102/17 and scored the first kill for the Fokker triplane on 7 September 1917.

LT Kurt Wolff was killed in action on 5 September 1917 in an engagement with British Sopwith Camels while flying F.I 102/17. The fabric, which covered the fuselage, wings and rudders was not painted, but was a pre-printed fabric.

A Fokker Dr. I (213/17) sits on the Fokker airfield at Schwerin-Goerries, awaiting delivery to a front line unit. When delivered from the factory, all production Dr. Is had their serial number painted on the fuselage side in Black.

This triplane (serial number unknown) was flown by LT Paul Baeumer, an ace with forty-four kills, while assigned to *Jasta* 2. Baeumer survived numerous combat engagements only to be killed on 15 July 1927 testing the Rohrbach Rofix fighter.

LT Kempf of *Jasta* 2 *Boelcke* poses with his Fokker Dr. I triplane. He scored his third victory over Grafenstafel on 20 October 1917, shooting down a British Sopwith Camel. The legend on the wing means "Do you know me yet?"

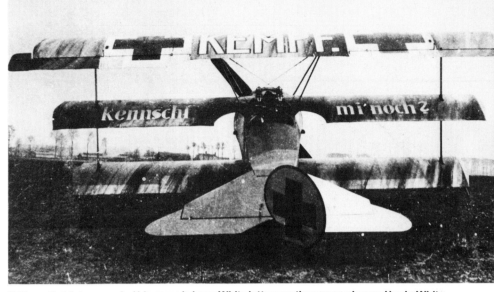

LT Kempf's triplane carried his name in large White letters on the upper wing and had a White tailplane. The legend on the middle wing was also in White against a dark Green background. Kempf's triplane also carried a large White K on the fuselage side.

This early production Fokker Dr. I (154/17) is parked on the Fokker airfield at Schwerin-Goerries. This aircraft was one of the third production batch which consisted of thirty aircraft.

A mechanic helps the pilot of a Fokker Dr. I strap into the cockpit in preparation for a patrol. Bad weather during the Winter of 1917/18 prevented *Jadgeschwader* 1 from undertaking large scale offensive patrols.

Fokker Dreidecker
Anschnallen des Kampffliegers vorm Start

1055
Photkartenvertrieb W.Sanke
BERLIN N.37.

15

CAPT Reinhardt became leader of *Jagdgeschwader* 1 after von Richthofen's death. Reinhardt's triplane was heavily damaged in combat during June of 1918, but he was able to make a successful landing. The tailplane was painted with Black and White stripes.

LT von Raben also was assigned to *Jasta* 7. His aircraft had a White rear fuselage and carried a White raven (Rabe) on the fuselage sides. Raben was shot down during 1918 and became a POW in France.

CAPT Reinhardt, one of the leading aces with twenty kills, poses alongside his damaged triplane. Reinhardt was another pilot who survived combat only to be killed in an accident. A few weeks after this forced landing, he was killed on 3 July 1918, testing the Dornier D.I at Adlershof.

LT Gontermann, leader of *Jasta* 15, poses with his brand new Dr. I (115/17) during October of 1917. The aircraft had just been delivered and had not been painted with his personal markings.

Fokker Dr. I (115/17) suffered an inflight failure of one of the ailerons, which led to complete failure of the upper wing. LT Gontermann was severely injured in the crash and died the next day of his injuries.

This Fokker Dr. I of *Jasta* 12 crashed after the wing failed in flight. The aileron separated from the aircraft causing complete failure of the upper wing. Such crashes caused the triplane to be grounded until new reinforced, waterproofed upper wings were manufactured.

Aileron

Dr. I

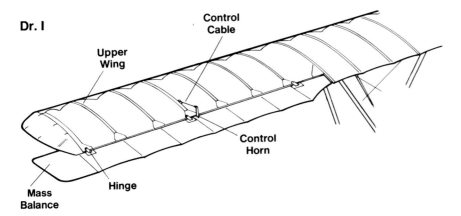

17

One of von Richthofen's Fokker Dr. Is (152/17) parked on the flight line of *Jasta* 5. It is clear that the undersides of the wings are a lighter color, believed to be Light Blue. This Dr. I was exhibited after the war at the *Zeughaus* (an armament museum) in Berlin, along with Boelcke's Fokker D III 352/16.

Manfred von Richthofen just before his last flight from Cappy airfield on 21 April 1918. The pilot with the dog is LT Loewenhardt of *Jasta* 11.

Lothar (left) and Manfred von Richthofen alongside a Dr. I triplane. Between them, the brothers downed 120 enemy aircraft. Manfred destroyed eighty aircraft while Lothar is credited with forty kills during a seventy-seven day period.

(Above) A lineup of Fokker Dr. Is assigned to *Jasta* 11 during March of 1918. The pilot with the walking stick is Manfred von Richthofen, commander of *Jadgeschwader* 1.

(Below) Lothar von Richthofen in the cockpit of his Red Dr. I triplane discusses an upcoming flight with other members of his squadron during early March of 1918.

Fokker Dr. I (425/17) was another of Manfred von Richthofen's Dr. Is. He scored his 80th victory in this aircraft on 20 April 20 1918, shooting down a Sopwith Camel. The combat report says only that this aircraft was painted Red, although the color of the wing undersurface appears to be Light Blue. Von Richthofen was killed later this same day in this aircraft.

Suffering from serious wounds, Lothar von Richthofen crash landed his triplane on 13 March near Awoingt. He was later killed flying as an air traffic pilot in a modified LVG C VI on 4 July 1922 near Hamburg.

LT Josef Jacobs (Pour le Merite) with the pilots of *Jasta* 7. Jacobs scored a total of forty-seven victories and was Germany's ninth ranking ace of the First World War.

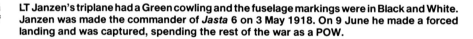

LT Johann Janzen of *Jasta* 6 in front of his triplane. The national insignia on the tail has a White border, while the remainder of the rudder has been painted in Green, the color of *Jasta* 6.

LT Janzen's triplane had a Green cowling and the fuselage markings were in Black and White. Janzen was made the commander of *Jasta* 6 on 3 May 1918. On 9 June he made a forced landing and was captured, spending the rest of the war as a POW.

(Above) This triplane belonged to LT Stapenhorst of *Jasta* 11. Stapenhorst scored four victories before being shot down and captured on 13 January 1918. The checkerboard marking on the fuselage was Black and White.

(Right) LT Erich Loewenhardt, leader of *Jasta* 10, poses in front of his Dr. I triplane. He scored a total of fifty-three victories before being killed in action on 10 August 1918. The decal on the propeller is the manufacturer's logo.

(Below) LT Stapenhorst's triplane was captured by the British when, during an attack on a kite balloon, he was surprised and forced down by British fighters. The checkerboard fuselage marking is Black and White, while the engine cowling is Red.

LT Steinhaeuser (10 victories, left) and LT Richard Wenzl (12 victories) of *Jasta 11* alongside Wenzl's Dr. I triplane. Steinhaeuser was killed in action on 26 June 1918 and Wenzl became the commander of *Jasta 4* on 20 October 1918.

This Dr. I triplane belonged to LT von Linsingen of *Jasta 11*. The engine cowling of the triplane was painted bright Red and the fuselage markings were Black and White.

CAPT Ritter von Tutschek, commander of *Jagdegeschwader* 2, in the cockpit of his Fokker Dr. I (404/17). Von Tutschek had the engine cowling of his triplane painted White, the same markings used on his earlier Albatros D.V.

Armament

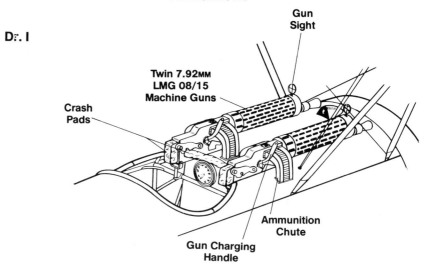

Dr. I

Gun Sight

Twin 7.92MM LMG 08/15 Machine Guns

Crash Pads

Ammunition Chute

Gun Charging Handle

(Above) This Fokker Dr. I is believed to be the first triplane assigned to *Jasta* 6. It is painted in the factory finish of Dark Green over Light Blue. The streaked appearance of the finish was caused by the method of painting; they were hand painted with three inch wide brushes.

Ritter von Tutschek poses with a captured British Spad VII (B6732) which he forced down in early March of 1918. His Fokker Dr. I (404/17) is parked in the background. Tutschek was killed in action on 15 March while flying with *Jasta* 23, after achieving a total of twenty-seven victories.

(Below) Executive Officer Otto Esswein of *Jasta* 26, in front of a lineup of *Jastsa* 26 triplanes. Esswein scored a total of twelve victories before he was killed in combat on 21 July 1918.

23

(Above) Triplanes of *Jasta* 11 parked on their field during the Spring of 1918. The forth triplane in line carries the White snake-line marking of LT Loewenhardt. He flew with *Jasta* 11 before he took command of *Jasta* 10.

(Below) A lineup of Fokker Dr. Is of *Jasta* 2 better known as *Jasta Boeloke* during May of 1918. The first aircraft in line is the triplane assigned to LT Kempf.

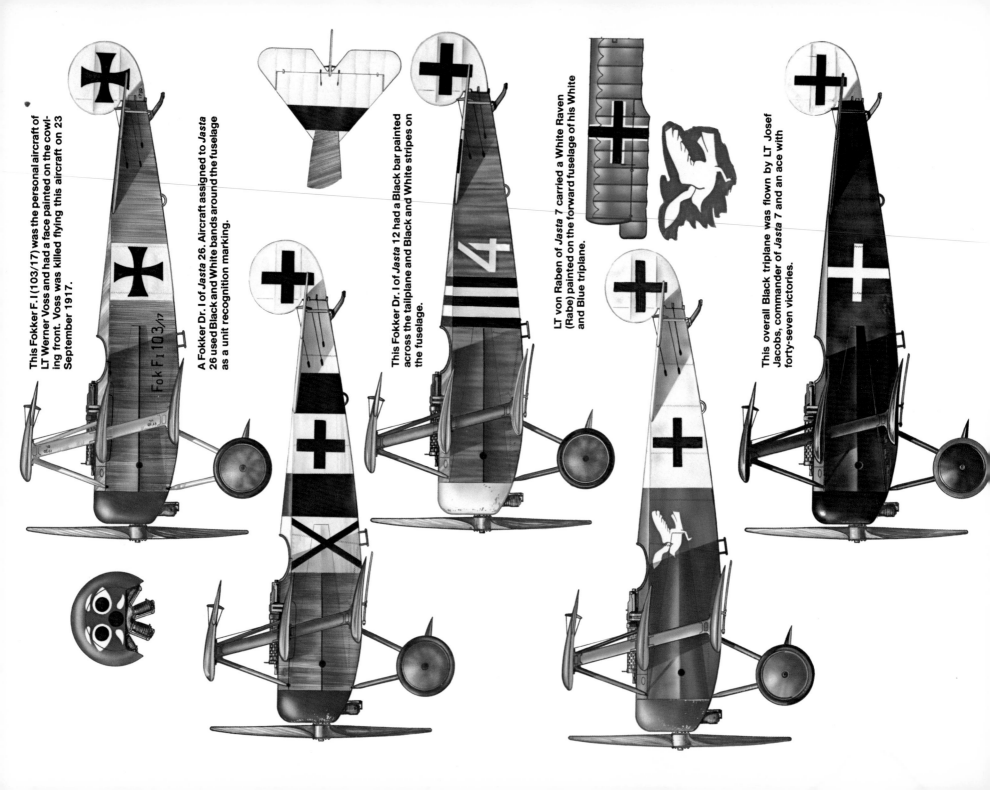

This Fokker F.I (103/17) was the personal aircraft of LT Werner Voss and had a face painted on the cowling front. Voss was killed flying this aircraft on 23 September 1917.

A Fokker Dr. I of Jasta 26. Aircraft assigned to Jasta 26 used Black and White bands around the fuselage as a unit recognition marking.

This Fokker Dr. I of Jasta 12 had a Black bar painted across the tailplane and Black and White stripes on the fuselage.

LT von Raben of Jasta 7 carried a White Raven (Rabe) painted on the forward fuselage of his White and Blue triplane.

This overall Black triplane was flown by LT Josef Jacobs, commander of Jasta 7 and an ace with forty-seven victories.

This Dr. I of *Jasta* 26 had Black and White bands around the entire rear fuselage including the tailplane.

Tail cross partially outlined

LT Paul Baeumer of *Jasta* 2 "*Boelcke*" flew this Dr. 1 (204/17). Baeumer was an ace with forty-four kills.

FoK DRiL

KEMPF

Cowl Face of Kempf's Dr. 1.

The Dr. I flown by LT Fritz Kempf was marked with his name in bold White letters on the center section of the upper wing.

This Dr. I was assigned to *Jasta* 2 during the Summer of 1918.

LT Kichstein of *Jasta* 6 flew this Dr. I painted overall White with diagonal Black stripes.

(Above) These triplanes are assigned to *Jasta* 26. The first aircraft from the left is that of CAPT Bruno Loerzer, commander of *Jadgeschwader* 3. His personal markings consisted of Black and White rings painted around the fuselage, the same markings he had used on his Albatros D.V.

(Below) Triplanes of *Jasta* 10 parked on the airfield at Lechelle (Somme) during March of 1918. The man with the tripod mounted glasses is standing watch for enemy aircraft, which often attacked German airfields in low level strafing attacks.

27

LT Hermann Goering in the cockpit of his Fokker Dr. I. Goering served as commander of *Jasta* 27. Later Goering took over command of *Jagdgeschwader* 1 and flew the Fokker D. VII. Goering had a holder for signal flares installed on the fuselage alongside the cockpit of his triplane.

LT Frommherz, who took over from Goering as squadron commander of *Jasta* 27, in the cockpit of his triplane. He scored a total of twenty-nine victories and survived the First World War.

LT Hermann Goering briefs pilots of *Jasta* 27 before a mission during June of 1918. Later Goering would become infamous as the leader of the Luftwaffe during the Second World War.

Signal Flare Holder

Dr. I

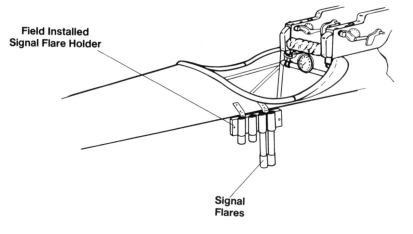

Field Installed
Signal Flare Holder

Signal
Flares

A Fokker Dr. I on final approach for landing at its home base. The curved cut-out in the middle wing was intended to gave the pilot an improved downward view.

LT Rudolf Stark, commander of *Jasta* 35, poses with his triplane which carries the later style *Balkenkruez* crosses on the fuselage side. Triplanes were repainted with these markings during the Spring of 1918.

These Dr. I triplanes of *Jadgeschwader* 1, are believed to be assigned to *Jasta* 10. All the aircraft are painted with bright Yellow engine cowlings as a unit recognition marking.

After returning from a mission, the triplanes of *Jasta* 12 were pushed to the maintenance tents by their ground crews. The triplane was easily maneuvered on the ground thanks to its light weight.

Triplanes of *Jasta* 12 are pushed across the soft landing ground of their airfield. *Jasta* 12 operated under the 5th Army in the Laon area during the Spring of 1918.

Three Non-commissioned Officer (NCO) pilots of *Jasta* 26 in front of their triplanes. (From left) Fritz Classen (ten victories), Otto Fruhner (twenty-eight victories) and Otto Esswein (twelve victories). The triplane in the foreground has a field installed five round signal flare holder on the fuselage alongside the cockpit.

Triplanes of *Jasta* 26 parked on their field at Sissonne during the Spring of 1918. The bands across the fuselage and tailplane of the triplane in the foreground are in Black and White.

(Above) A Fokker triplane of *Jagdgeschwader* 1 flies low over its landing ground just after takeoff. The triplane could be airborne after a takeoff run of some one hundred and fifty feet.

(Below) The triplanes of *Jasta* 26 had the cowlings painted in bright Yellow. The aircraft in the foreground has four White bars painted on the fuselage sides just behind the cockpit, while the aircraft behind it has a White bar on the fuselage side.

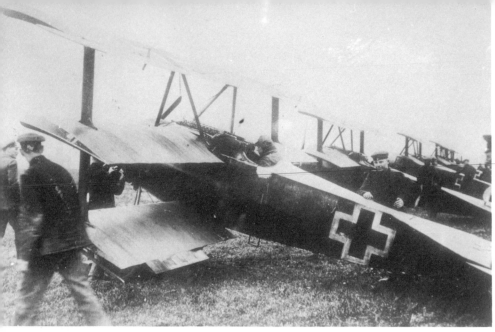

Fokker Dr. Is of *Jasta* 26 are prepared by their ground crews for takeoff from Sissonne during the *Battle of France* in the Spring of 1918.

Ground crews of *Jagdgeschwader* 3 wait near their triplanes for the order to takeoff. The small attachment on the fuselage alongside the cockpit of the triplane in the foreground is a holder for signal flares, a common field modification on Dr. Is.

LT Loeffler poses in front of his Fokker Dr. I. He was assigned to *Jasta* 2 (*Boelcke*) which was under the tactical control of *Jagdgeschwader* 3. He scored a total of fifteen victories and survived the war.

LT Pastor of *Jasta* 11, in the cockpit of his Fokker Dr. I (121/17). He was killed in a crash near Moorseele on 31 October 1917, when his Dr. I suffered structural failure of the upper wing. His crash was one of several that resulted in the grounding of the Dr. I.

Ground crews steady the wings of a Dr. I of *Jasta* 12 as it taxis over the uneven grass landing ground. The triplane had a tendency to dip a wing when taxiing because of its narrow track undercarriage.

Ground crews of *Jagdgeschwader* 1 prepare a Fokker Dr. I for its next mission. One mechanic appears to be adjusting the engine while another waits to pull the propeller through to start the engine.

A Fokker Dr. I of *Jasta* 10 parked on the landing ground of the squadron's base at Avesnes-le-sec during March of 1918. It is believed that the fuselage bands are Black and White.

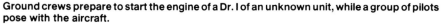

Ground crews prepare to start the engine of a Dr. I of an unknown unit, while a group of pilots pose with the aircraft.

A Fokker Dr. I triplane on the airfield at Fl.ABt (A) 224. The circular emblem on the propeller is the logo of the propeller's manufacturer, Axial Propeller fabric A.G. of Berlin.

The twin air-cooled 7.92ᴍᴍ LMG 08/15 machine guns were fed via chutes from two ammunition boxes in the fuselage. The guns could be fired either singly or together. This pilot has added a rear view mirror to the starboard rear cabane strut of his Fokker.

Field Installed Rear View Mirror

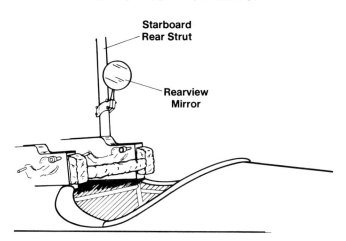

Starboard
Rear Strut

Rearview
Mirror

A Fokker Dr. I of *Jagdgeschwader* 1 parked outside the unit maintenance hangar. *Jagdeschwader* 1 was the first unit in the German Army Air Service to receive the triplane and flew it longer than any other unit.

Corporal Beschow, a non-commission pilot of *Jasta* 6, poses in front of his triplane. He was assigned to *Jasta* 6 on 23 September 1917 and was wounded in action on 10 March 1918. During his entire tour with the unit he did not score a single victory.

This triplane was flown by Victor Lobbe, who was an instructor attached to the *Jastadschule* (fighter school) at Nivelles. The man standing next to the Fokker Dr. I (565/17) on 18 January 1918 is one of his student pilots.

Max Schueler built this Fokker Dr. I copy under the designation Vagel Grip Sp 3. The aircraft was registered and flown as a civil sport aircraft with the civil registration number D 664. Schueler used the aircraft primarily for advertising flights throughout Germany.

These Dr. I. replicas were painted in various unit markings to represent German aces and front line units for the movie *D III 88*.

This Fokker Dr. I replica was one of two built after 1933 by Alfred Friedrich in Straussberg (near Berlin) for use in the filming of a movie. After the film was completed this aircraft was donated to the Berlin Air Museum where it was destroyed during the Second World War.

Vicefeldwebel Willy Gabriel, a former member of *Jasta* 11 with eleven victories, flew this Fokker Dr. I replica in the movie *D III 88*. It was the second aircraft produced by Alfred Friedrich.

Fokker Experimental Triplanes

During the course of the war Fokker continued to experiment with triplane designs aimed at improving the Dr. I. The Germans realized that the 110 hp rotary engine of the Dr. I was somewhat underpowered and attempted improvements in the area of engine power. A number of different engines were tried out in modified Dr. Is to test these power plant configurations.

Fokker V.6

One experimental prototype was built in an attempt to mate the Dr. I airframe with the Mercedes in-line engine. The Fokker V.6 prototype was basically a Dr. I airframe modified to mount the 160 hp Mercedes D III liquid-cooled in-line engine. To install the Mercedes engine it was necessary to enlarge the Dr. I airframe to absorb the increased power. The wing span was increased to 26 feet 6 inches and the forward fuselage was lengthened in front of the cockpit.

The frontal engine radiator used on the V.6 prototype proved superior to the wing mounted engine radiators of other German fighters and was used successfully on the Fokker D VII.

Initially the lower wing was mounted a short distance below the lower fuselage, which resulted in a large gap between the wing surface and the fuselage. During testing, it was found that this configuration had serious aerodynamic problems. The wing/fuselage gap caused interference drag, premature flow separation over the wing surface, and an excessive vortex region over the tailplane, reducing its effectiveness drastically. To improve the aircraft's aerodynamics and reduce drag, the wing/fuselage gap was faired over, which added to the aircraft's depth and fuselage side area.

Flight tests with the modified V.6 quickly revealed that it was far less maneuverable than the standard Dr. I and, because of the lengthened nose, the pilot's view from the cockpit was poor. As a result of these unfavorable pilot reports, Fokker decided to abandon further development of the aircraft.

One feature of the V.6 that was to find favor in later Fokker designs was the nose mounted radiator. The positioning of the engine radiator immediately behind the propeller was far superior to other German in-line powered fighters which mounted the radiators on the wing surfaces. This nose mounted radiator configuration was used successfully in the later Fokker D.VII.

Fokker V.7

At least four triplane prototypes were built by Fokker with the designation Fokker V.7. All were standard Dr. I airframes modified to accept different rotary engine power plants of varying horsepower.

The Siemens und Halske company completed their experimental Sh.3 eleven cylinder 160 hp geared rotary engine during late 1917 and Fokker received an order for one experimental prototype Dr. I which was to be powered by the Sh.3.

The Fokker V.7 (1788) was a standard Dr. I airframe modified to mount the Sh.3. To mount this new engine, the engine mounts were modified and the cowling slightly enlarged. The prototype was fitted with a larger diameter four blade propeller. To provide the necessary ground clearance for the larger four blade propeller the undercarriage legs were lengthened and the airfoil fairing between the struts removed.

Tests with the prototype revealed that it was ungainly on the ground and difficult to taxi, due to the increased height of the nose. Performance on and near the ground was also impaired. The prototype did show improvement in both climb and altitude performance, although the test pilots reported that it was sensitive on the controls and slightly unstable; perhaps too unstable for the average fighter pilot at the front. Landing and approach required care and even with the center landing gear airfoil fairing deleted, the V.7 still had a tendency to float near the ground. The torque from the four blade propeller was also a problem because of the aircraft's overall short wing span.

While flight tests were being conducted, engine ground tests revealed that the Sh.3 was not ready for front line service. There were problems with the pistons and the only oil available proved unsuitable for the engine. In the event, the *IdFlieg* felt that the aircraft was unsuitable for front line service and it was not ordered into production.

A second V.7 prototype, 1830, was built to study the Dr. Is performance when powered by a 160 hp rotary engine. It is believed that the engine fitted was a twin-row fourteen cylinder 160 hp Obersursel U III rotary engine. The prototype was retained at the Fokker factory and after completing its testing, the aircraft was given the service designation Dr. I 100/17 and delivered to *Jagdstaffelschule II* on 22 May 1918.

The Fokker V.6 was an enlarged version of the V.4 prototype fitted with a 120 hp in-line water cooled Mercedes engine. The heavier V.6 lacked the performance of the Dr. I and further development was abandoned.

The third V.7 (1919) was powered by a 170 hp Goebel Goe III rotary engine and took part in the fighter competition of January 1919. To compensate for the additional weight of the more powerful engine, the fuselage was lengthened by some twenty-one inches. During the competition, the V.7 demonstrated a definite improvement in climb and altitude performance over the standard Dr. I; however, the engine failed to develop its full power and on its last flight, three cylinders failed. Fuel consumption was also reported to be higher than that of other engines with comparable horsepower.

In the event, the engine failed to perform to expectations and did not enter production. The prototype was later designated Dr. I 599/17 and its ultimate fate remains unknown.

The last V.7 prototype (1981) was ordered in October of 1917. The aircraft was powered by a Steyr-built 145 hp rotary engine and had the same fuselage extension as V.7 1919. It was intended that the V.7 would compete in the 1918 Austro-Hungarian Fighter Evaluation; however, the aircraft was severely damaged in a landing accident on one of its early test flights. Since it could not be repaired in time for the competition, the prototype was written off and scrapped.

At least three Dr. Is (485/17, 527/17 and 562/17) were fitted with captured 130 hp French built Clerget rotary engines for test purposes. These aircraft were never intended for operational use and were used solely for investigation of the captured engine's performance and potential. Some of the tests involved operation with German *ersatz* (synthetic) castor oil to determine if these engines could operate effectively with this oil. As with German engines, the oil was found to cause overheating problems with these engines as well.

The last engine experiments involved fitting standard Dr. I airframes with supercharged rotary engines. One such aircraft was powered by a Oberursel II engine fitted with a Schwade gear driven compresser. The compresser was mounted behind the engine alongside the crankshaft and carburetor. Although successfully test flown, the war ended before the engine/supercharger combination could go into production.

One other attempt at improving the speed of the Dr. I was undertaken during April of 1918. Five production Dr. Is were each covered with a silk fabric replacing the standard cloth coverings. These aircraft were sent to *Jadgeschwder* 1 for evaluation where it was found that the silk stayed taut longer, oil was more easily cleaned from the wing surfaces, and the aircraft were faster. By this time, however, operational use of the Dr. I was nearly at its end; however, and recovering the remaining triplanes with silk fabric was not undertaken.

The Fokker V.7 (1788) was a standard Dr. I airframe fitted with a 160 hp radial engine and longer undercarriage legs to provide the necessary ground clearance for the large four blade propeller.

This V.7 prototype (1981) was fitted with an eleven cylinder 145 hp Steyr-built Le Rhone radial engine which was housed in an enlarged cowling with additional cooling vents. The aircraft was intended for the Austro-Hungarian Fighter Evaluations at Aspern held during July of 1918, but crashed prior to the evaluations.

Nose Development

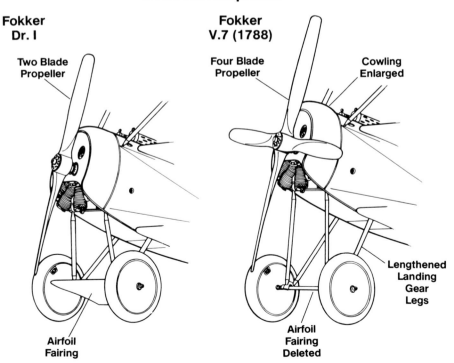

Fokker
Dr. I

Two Blade
Propeller

Airfoil
Fairing

Fokker
V.7 (1788)

Four Blade
Propeller

Cowling
Enlarged

Lengthened
Landing
Gear
Legs

Airfoil
Fairing
Deleted

This Dr. I is believed to be one of five aircraft built with silk fabric replacing the standard linen fabric used on the Dr. I. The aircraft were tested in combat where they were reported to be somewhat faster than a standard Dr. I and easier to maintain.

Fokker Competitors

The appearance of the Sopwith Triplane during April of 1917 and its outstanding performance resulted in what has come to be known as the "triplane craze" among German aircraft designers. After evaluation of a captured Sopwith Triplane confirmed the Sopwith's superiority over the current generation of German fighters, the German Army Air Service invited a number of companies to submit triplane designs for consideration.

After the success of the Fokker Dr. I, a number of German manufactures also produced triplane designs in order to compete with the Dr. I for production orders from the German Army Air Service. In the event, none of these designs proved successful and the Dr. I remained the only front line triplane fighter to see wide spread service in the German Army Air Service.

A.E.G. Dr. I

A.E.G. introduced their triplane fighter prototype, the A.E.G. Dr. I, during October of 1917. The aircraft, basically a triplane configuration of the earlier A.E.G. D.I fighter, proved to be slower than the standard D.I and offered no improvement in climb performance. After these disappointing test results, further development of the aircraft was abandoned.

A.E.G. PE

The A.E.G. PE was an armored triplane ground attack aircraft which was submitted for testing during early 1918. The aircraft featured a metal sparred wing and a metal skinned armored fuselage. The aircraft remained purely an experimental design and no production was ever undertaken.

Albatros Dr. I

The Albatros Dr. I was a triplane conversion of the standard Albatros D. V airframe intended to compete with the Fokker Dr. I during the 1917 *IdFlieg* fighter evaluations. The three wings were of parallel chord, and ailerons, with connecting steel link struts, were installed on all three wings. Early flight tests revealed its performance offered no improvement over the standard Albatros D.V and was far inferior to the Fokker Dr. I. The tests were halted when the aircraft experienced engine cooling problems and further development was abandoned.

The Sopwith Triplane began the "Triplane Craze" within the German Army Air Service. This aircraft was captured by the Germans after it was forced down by LT von Schoenebeck of *Jasta* 11 on 27 July 1917. The aircraft was repainted in German markings and test flown. A second Sopwith was forced down by LT Wuesthoff of *Jasta* 4 on 13 September 1917.

Albatros Dr. II

Another unsuccessful effort by Albatros to build a competitive triplane fighter was the Albatros Dr. II built during 1918. The aircraft consisted of a Albatros D.X airframe powered by a 195 hp Benz IVb V-8 engine. The wings were installed in a staggered layout, braced by wide parallel I struts. The combination of these struts and the wing mounted engine radiators caused considerable drag and the aircraft's performance was reportedly poor. Like the earlier Dr. I, the project was cancelled.

D.F.W. Dr. I

The D.F.W. Dr. I was entered in the 1918 fighter competition held at Adlershof and was a triplane variant of the earlier D.F.W. D.I (which was also entered into the same competition). The aircraft was powered by a 160 hp Mercedes D III in-line water cooled engine. By this time, the German Army Air Service had lost interest in triplane fighters and the competition was won by Fokker with the prototype of the biplane D. VII.

Euler Triplanes

The Euler company built several unsuccessful triplane designs including the Dr. I, Dr. II, Dr. III, and Dr. IV (although these designations were never officially assigned to these aircraft).

The Dr. I was a very portly aircraft powered by a 160 hp Oberursel U III rotary engine. The Dr. II was an experimental triplane fighter powered by a 160 hp Mercedes D III in-line water cooled engine. The Dr. III was a development of the Dr. II fitted with a 100 hp Obersurel U I rotary engine. This aircraft closely resembled the Fokker Dr. I and several references have been made suggesting that it was a copy of the Fokker Dr. I with a modified rudder and a dorsal fin.

The last Euler triplane was the Dr. IV. Built during 1916, the Dr. IV was intended as a training aircraft and featured side-by-side seating for the instructor and student. The aircraft was powered by a 220 hp Mercedes D IV in-line water cooled engine driving a four blade propeller. As with the earlier triplane designs submitted by Euler, the type failed to find favor with the *IdFlieg* and did not enter production.

Pfalz Dr. I and Dr. II

The Pfalz Dr. I was basically a Pfalz D VII biplane fighter outfitted with a set of triplane wings. The aircraft was built during the Fall of 1917 and was officially tested in October of that year. The aircraft was powered by an eleven cylinder 160 hp Siemens-Halske Sh III rotary engine enclosed in a circular aluminum cowling with twelve cooling vents. The wings were of unequal span and chord and were fitted with ailerons on the top wing.

During December of 1917 the Pfalz company invited Manfred von Richtohfen to inspect and test fly the aircraft as a possible replacement for the Fokker Dr. I. Von Richthofen and Adolf Ritter von Tutschek (who was recovering from a shoulder wound) visited the Pfalz factory and both pilots flew the prototype. Their flight tests revealed that its performance was adequate; however, its handling qualities were rated as inferior to those of the Fokker Dr. I and the engine did not produce its full horsepower. These test results did not justify large scale production, although the Bavarian government ordered limited production of the type for Bavarian units. No records exist that give exact production figures for the Pfalz Dr. I; however, it is believed that at least ten aircraft were produced and saw limited service.

At least one Pfalz Dr. II was built and tested. This aircraft differed from the Dr. I in the engine and cowling, being fitted with a 100 hp Oberursel rotary engine housed in an open cowling. Later the Dr. II was re-engined with a 110 hp Sh I rotary under the designation Dr. IIa. Neither type was put into production.

The AEG Dr. I triplane was actually a standard AEG D.I modified to the triplane configuration with new wings. Tests revealed that the aircraft had no increase in climb performance and its speed was reduced.

Another AEG triplane design was the AEG PE (*Panzer-Einsitzer*), an armored single seat fighter intended as a ground support aircraft. The prototype featured metal sparred wings and a metal skinned armored fuselage.

Another Pfalz undesignated experimental triplane fighter was built during 1917. This aircraft was basically a conversion of an existing fighter to the triplane configuration to test the performance of the type as a triplane. One Pfalz D III fighter airframe was experimentally fitted with a third short chord wing mounted high on the fuselage between the standard biplane wings. The aircraft was powered by a 160 hp Mercedes in-line engine and was completed; however, it reportedly never actually flew.

Siemens-Schuckert Dr. I

The Siemens-Schuckert Dr. I was a highly unusual single seat twin engine triplane fighter, which became known as the "Flying Egg". It was powered by two 120 hp Sh Ia radial engines in a push-pull (tractor/pusher) arrangement. The front engine (tractor) drove a two blade propeller while the rear (pusher) engine drove a four blade propeller. The tail assembly, with a single elevator and twin rudders, was mounted on tubular outrigger booms which attached to the trailing edges of the top and bottom wings. The fuselage consisted of a tub which was suspended on struts between the upper and lower wings, with the third wing being attached to the fuselage tub. The aircraft reportedly crashed on its maiden flight during November of 1917 and was not rebuilt. A further development of the Dr. I, the Dr. II was to be powered by two Sh III engines; however, the project was cancelled before a prototype was built.

Other known unsuccessful triplane designs include the Brandenburg L 16 experimental triplane fighter; L.F.G. Roland D IV triplane fighter powered by a 190 hp engine; the Sablatnig SF 4, a triplane fighter mounted on floats; and the Schütte-Lanz Dr. I triplane fighter prototype.

Albatros used a standard D V airframe converted to a triplane configuration as its entry into the 1917 fighter competition. The aircraft offered no advantage over the standard D.V and further development was abandoned.

The DFW Dr. I triplane fighter prototype during tests at Adlershof during 1918. The aircraft proved to be unacceptable and was not ordered into production.

Another Albatros triplane project was the Dr. II, a triplane version of the experimental Albatros D. X fighter. Its performance was a disappointment and further development of triplanes at Albatros was cancelled.

44

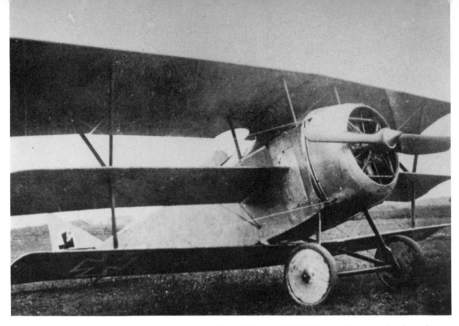

The Euler Dr. I triplane prototype was produced during 1916. The rather portly aircraft was powered by a 160 hp Oberursel U III rotary engine.

The Euler Dr. II was powered by a 160 hp Mercedes in-line water cooled engine. The engine cooling radiators were mounted along the fuselage side.

Euler's Dr. III prototype closely resembled the Fokker Dr. I with the exception of the rudder and dorsal fin. The aircraft was a development of the Dr. I and was powered by a 100 hp Oberursel U I rotary engine.

The Euler Dr. IV was designed by August Euler, of Frankfurt during 1915 as a two seat trainer aircraft with side-by-side seating for the instructor and student.

The Pfalz Dr. I (3050/17), was flight tested by von Richthofen and Tutschek at the Pfalz factory in Speyer during October of 1917. It is believed that ten aircraft were produced and saw limited service.

Mechanics work on the Pfalz Dr. II (left) parked next to the Pfalz Dr. I on the factory airfield at Speyer during factory testing. The Dr. II was powered by a 100 hp Oberursel rotary engine housed in an open cowling.

During 1917, Pfalz also tried to modify the standard Pfalz D III fighter biplane to a triplane configuration by adding a third wing between the standard biplane wings. Reportedly, the aircraft never flew.

The push-pull Siemens-Schuckert Dr. I crashed on its first flight and development of the aircraft was abandoned. Known as the "Flying Egg," it failed to match the performance of the Fokker Dr. I and was not ordered into production.

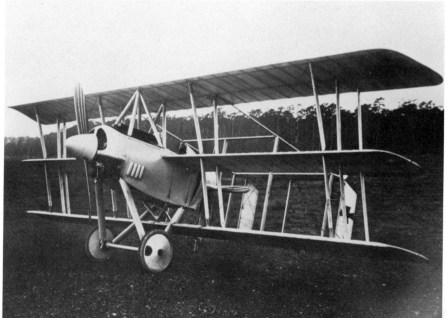

Fokker Replicas

Although today no original Fokker Dr. Is exist, a great number of replica Fokker Dr. Is have been built. The majority of these aircraft use the 185 hp Warner Scarab radial engine; however, there was at least one replica know to be flying using a 100 hp Gnome rotary engine.

Replica Dr. Is have been noted on the civil registers of Germany, Britain, Singapore and the United States, where at least twenty replicas have been built. One of the most popular Fokker Dr. I replicas is produced both in plans and in a home-built kit by the Ron Sands Inc. By late January of 1986, some 120 sets of full sized plans and ten kits had been sold, with a total of eighteen aircraft flying. The Sands replica plans recommend the use of a 150-180 hp Lycoming engine, with either a Warner or Le rhone nine cylinder radial engine as alternate power plants. Performance figures include a top speed of 120 mph and a ceiling of 15,000 feet.

One Dr. I replica, regularly flown in the US, is powered by a 220 hp Continental engine which, at double the horsepower of the original, gives this particular triplane truly outstanding performance.

Mr. Randy Wilson of Dallas, Texas, owns one Sands replica and regularly flies this aircraft in airshows. He has prepared a pilot's handbook for the aircraft and the following comments on the handling of the Fokker Dr. I replica are extracted from this handbook.

As in all triplanes, the position of the middle wing leaves the pilot blind on the ground. The only view forward is by looking underneath the wing via the cutouts on each side of the cockpit. Needless to say, S-turns during taxi are mandatory. All that wing area makes the plane sensitive to moderate winds even on the ground, so don't get in a hurry taxing. For takeoff, keep the stick in the neutral position or slightly back and apply power slowly. Raise the tail gently, but positively, into a level flight attitude. Acceleration is rapid and engine torque is very noticeable with the application of the last half of the throttle, but easily controlled with right rudder. Liftoff will be at about 55-60 mph.

One of the "Blue Max" movie pilots described the flying characterics of the replicas used in that movie as having the flying characteristics of a Link trainer. The alierons are somewhat heavy, but the rudder and elevator are light and positive. The aircraft will stall at about 40 mph with a moderate wing drop. If the stall is abrupt, the break is sharp and there is a tendency to roll inverted. Loops are very easily performed from 100 mph, but must be kept tight.

Triplanes probably have the worst reputation of any WW I plane for nasty landing habits, and in fact, some of this is deserved. Most important is to be sure and keep the wings level and DON'T BOUNCE IT! If you get a good bounce out of the plane while trying a full-stall, three point landing, you have an excellent chance of banging a lower wingtip into the ground. That is what the wingtip skids were out there for on the original.

Wilson's replica is not fitted with a radio, because the Werner Scarab engine fitted to the replica is unshielded. Besides the Scarab engine, the aircraft also differs from an original Dr. I in having wheel brakes and a tail wheel in place of the tail skid found on original Dr. Is. His aircraft is also fitted with a smoke system for airshow work. One interesting thing is that this replica has a data plate on the engine firewall from an original Fokker Dr. I.

Although tricky to fly and not for the average sport pilot, the Dr. I triplane remains a popular subject for home-builders and triplane replicas can be expected to be regular performers at air shows for years to come.

This Dr. 1 replica was under construction in West Germany during 1966. The aircraft was destined for display in a museum.

The completed Dr. I replica before loading in a Lufthansa Boeing B 707 for delivery to a museum. The aircraft is painted to represent one of von Richtofen's Dr. Is.

A number of replica Dr. Is have been built both for commercial and sport use. This ¾ scale Dr.I replica was built in the United States as a home-built project and was used on the airshow circuit.

One of the American built Fokker Dr. I replicas in flight at an air show. The triplane is a popular home-built project in the United States where at least twenty are known to be flying.

This Fokker Dr. I replica is owned and flown by Mr. Randy Wilson in the Dallas/Ft Worth, Texas area. The aircraft is powered by a Warner Scarab radial engine and has a data plate from an original Fokker Dr. I on the engine firewall. (Nicholas J. Waters III)

Mr. Wilson's Dr. I differs from an original Fokker triplane in having a tail wheel instead of a tail skid. The aircraft is also equipped with wheel brakes and a smoke system for air show work. (Nicholas J. Waters III)

The Dr. I replica instrument panel contains several instruments not found on an original Fokker. A slip meter is installed between the guns and the aircraft also has a G meter installed.

The wingtip skids on the Wilson replica are made from ax handles and differ in shape from those installed on original Dr. Is. The aircraft is painted to represent von Richthofen's Dr. I 127/17, his last triplane. (Nicholas J. Waters III)

According to Mr. Wilson, the ailerons on the Dr. I replica are somewhat heavy, while the rudder and elevators are light and very positive. The aircraft is somewhat tricky to fly and is not recommended for the average sport pilot. (Nicholas J. Waters III)

The overall Red finish on the Wilson Dr. I replica is extremely smooth and glossy. The aircraft is always extremely popular with the crowd at any airshow in which it is flown. (Nicholas J. Waters III)

Other German Aircraft
from squadron/signal

1044

1057

1085

1113

 **squadron/signal publications**